A Sloth for all Seasons

Deep in the Rainforest in Brazil in South America lives Simon, the happy and friendly sloth. Look closely, can you see him? Simon is there, but let us take a closer look.

Can you see Simon now? Of course, he is hanging upside down from a branch of a tree in the background. Let us get even closer and see what he is doing. He might be talking to other animals.

"Hello, Toucan," said Simon, "I am going to leave this forest. I want to know what it is like to have a cold and snowy winter. I want a spring when flowers carpet the ground and the scent of blossoms fill the air. I want a dry and sunny summer, and I also want autumn when leaves in many of the trees change colour and fall to the ground."

"But you love it here, and we will miss you, Simon," said the toucan. Simon looked sad and said, "Yes, I will miss you too, I will miss all of my forest friends, but we only seem to get two seasons here in the rainforest. One of which is the rainy season, and the other is the dry season. It can rain too much in both seasons, and it is always hot.
Page 4

Simon and the toucan gave each other a big hug and said goodbye. The toucan knew that it was important for Simon to experience four seasons in other parts of the world.

Simon travelled from deep in the forest to a big city near the sea where he had a clever plan. He knew he would not be able to buy a plane ticket, and Simon had no passport, so he lay on a chair, pretending to be a cute, cuddly toy, hoping that a child would pick him up and take him on a plane to Europe.

Sure enough, a little while later, a young girl could not believe her luck to see what looked like a toy Sloth, and she thought the sloth had been left and forgotten. So, she decided to take Simon on the plane with her. Simon's plan worked perfectly. He was on his way to Europe.

Simon had never been on a plane and had never sat on a chair. So, he climbed up on the side of a chair and was extremely comfortable. But, of course, the little girl could not believe what Simon was doing. She still thought he was just a cuddly toy.

It was a cold and wet autumn day when they landed in the United Kingdom. Simon told the girl that he was a real sloth and wanted to experience the seasons in Europe. The little girl was sad but understood. Finally, they said goodbye to each other.

Thankfully for Simon, it was not always raining. It seemed that when there are four seasons, each season is about three months long. So, it meant there would be lots of dry and sunny days for Simon to enjoy, although it was much colder than his forest home.

Simon had fun playing in the leaves. Leaves fell in his home forest, but they usually turned damp and mushy quickly on the dark and wet forest floor. So, Simon found it wonderful to see leaves that were often very dry and fun to play in. Can you see him in the leaves?

"Hi, what are you?" Asked Simon to the strange-looking creature on the ground. "I am a fox," said the fox. "Oh, I have never seen a fox before. I have also never seen anything like what is going on over there. What is it?" Asked Simon.

"In many countries, autumn is the time to celebrate Halloween, a tradition that dates back many years, when people celebrated saints, who were deeply religious, holy people. These days, most people dress up in scary costumes, collect candy and have fun," said the fox.

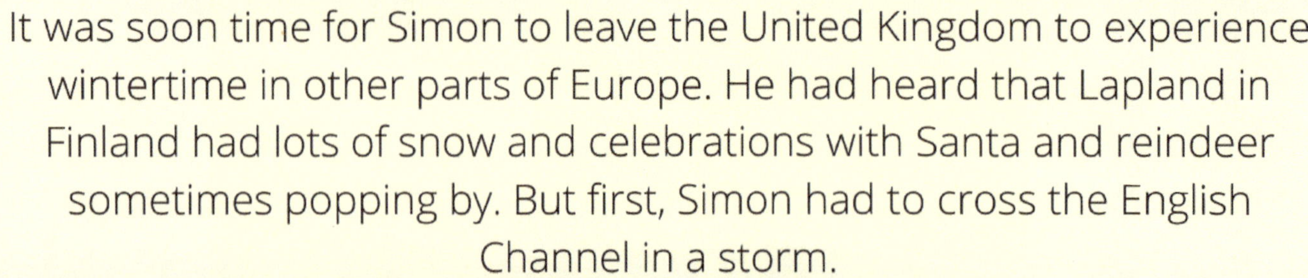

It was soon time for Simon to leave the United Kingdom to experience wintertime in other parts of Europe. He had heard that Lapland in Finland had lots of snow and celebrations with Santa and reindeer sometimes popping by. But first, Simon had to cross the English Channel in a storm.

Later that day, Simon arrived on a beach in France. The stormy weather had turned to sunshine. Simon asked a hermit crab, "Hi hermit crab, how do I get to Lapland from here?" The crab looked at Simon and said, "You have a long way to go. Get on a bus or train."

Simon accepted the crab's advice and went to a bus station, where he was surprised to see other animals from around the world. "What are you all doing here?" Asked Simon. "We are here to experience each of the four seasons in Europe, just like you," said the monkey.

Soon, the bus arrived, and all the animals got on. The other animals were not all going to Lapland in the north. They wanted to experience the four seasons in different ways. There was an excellent time to be had in every European country.

Simon would have loved to have seen more countries in Europe, but it would have taken him far too long. Still, Simon chose countries to the west, north, east, and south, and he would pass through many other countries along the way.

In Lapland, Simon stayed in an empty house, which he had all to himself. Then, days later, it was Christmas Eve, and Simon fell fast asleep by the fire. The following day just before he was due to leave, he had the most beautiful surprise.

Not only had there been snow on the ground when Simon arrived, but it had now started to snow. And that was not all! Santa had arrived with Rudolph, the red-nosed reindeer, to wish Simon a Merry Christmas. Simon was happy, and it was time to board the bus.

Simon travelled east and south through beautiful winter countryside and exciting countries for several days and nights. Finally, he hoped to reach a country named Greece, where he planned to relax for a little while and enjoy spring.

Simon arrived in Greece, where he spent time relaxing and looking forward to Easter and waiting for spring to arrive. Soon enough, it was spring. The trees were full of flowers and leaves, and the ground was alive with flowers and plants.

"Hello, little sloth," said a young Greek girl with her donkey. Are you enjoying Easter and spring?" "Oh yes," said Simon, "but tomorrow I am heading west to Spain for summer before returning home."

The next day, Simon was on his way to Spain. On his way, he sailed from Greece to Italy, where he then boarded a train and travelled along the coast of Italy, Monaco, and southern France, which was fun. However, he took his time, as he was too early for summer.

After quite some time, Simon arrived in Spain. "What are you going to do now?" Asked the train driver. "I am going to visit some beautiful cities and towns and other landmarks. Then I am going to sit on the beach and enjoy hot and sunny and dry weather," said Simon.

As Simon lay on a lovely Spanish beach, he thought about everything he had seen and experienced while enjoying four seasons in Europe. Although he had a great time, he missed his home and friends and could not wait to return to his forest.

Pretending to be a toy worked so well on the first plane to the United Kingdom, so Simon played the same trick to get on the plane home. Simon also learned that he should sit on seats and not climb all over them, and it was much more comfortable.

Simon made his way back home, and he was happy. It was great to experience other things, but there was no place like home, and he loved his forest. He did not rule out any future adventures, but he was happy where he was, for now.

Simon's Map
N
W E
S
NORWAY
SWEDEN
FINDLAND
RUSSIA
ESTONIA
LATVIA
LITHUANIA
IRELAND
UNITED KINGDOM
DENMARK
NETHERLAND
BELGIUM
GERMANY
POLAND
BELORUSSIA
FRANCE
CZECH REPUBLIC
SLOVAKIA
UKRAINE
SWITZERLAND
AUSTRIA
HUNGARY
MOLDOVA
SLOVENIA
ITALY
CROATIA
ROMANIA
PORTUGAL
SPAIN
BOSNIA
SERBIA
MACEDONIA
BULGARIA
MONTENEGRO
YUGOSLAVIA
ALBANIA
GREECE
Page 29

SLOTH FUN FACTS

Sloths live in the wild in Central and South America across several hot, humid and wet countries with lots of thick vegetation, which is every sloth's preferred place to live.

There are two types of sloth, the two-toed sloth and the three-toed sloth, and there are six species. It is funny, but all species of sloth have three toes, but only the two-toed sloth has two fingers.

Extinct species of sloths are said to have been much larger than a car. Thankfully, these days sloths are smaller than an average-sized dog.

One of the reasons sloths are so slow is that the buds, fruits and leaves they eat can take a whole month to digest in their four stomachs. That process tires them out just by eating enough food to keep them alive, so they save energy by moving slowly. Very slowly.

Sloths move slowly in the hot and humid climate, so many other creatures make homes in a sloth's thick fur, including fleas, beetles, moths, as well as green algae and fungi.

Sloths, on average, go to the toilet just once a week, and they climb down out of the trees to do it.

Sloths also have long tongues, at about as long as a school ruler.